This book belongs to:

_____

# The Girl Who Protected Welwitschia Mirabilis, The Great & Giant Plant in Angola

MUÌJI YA KINLUNJI
(MARIA SANTANA)

Copyright © 2024 by Muìji Ya Kinlunji (Maria Santana)

Paperback: 978-1-965632-68-0
eBook: 978-1-965632-69-7
Library of Congress Control Number: 2024924178

All rights reserved. No part of this publication may be reproduced, distributed, or transmitted in any form or by any electronic or mechanical means, without the prior written permission of the publisher, except in the case of brief quotations embodied in critical reviews and certain other noncommercial uses permitted by copyright law.

This Book is a work of fiction. Names, characters, places, and incidents either are the product of the author's imagination or are used fictitiously. Any resemblance to actual persons, living or dead, events, or locales is entirely coincidental.

Ordering Information:

Prime Seven Media
518 Landmann St.
Tomah City, WI 54660

Printed in the United States of America

# Other Books by the Author

-  A Precol do Meu Tempo

- A Palanca Mas Cobiçada de Angola

# Table of Contents

# Intro

Luna, a curious girl who cares about nature, returns to school after the blue summer and discovers that the rare Mutumbu plant, found only in Angola, is in danger. Together with her classmates and under the guidance of her teacher, they learn about the importance of environmental conservation and write a letter to the Minister of the Environment. This exciting and educational story highlights the power of children to protect the environment and the importance of preserving the natural wonders of our planet.

# Prologue

In the small village where Luna lived, everything around her stirred her curiosity and concern. With her kind heart and attentive gaze, she observed nature and the people, always seeking to understand and protect the world around her. After the blue summer, Luna returned to school with mixed feelings. While her classmates shared exciting adventures, Luna had a different story to tell.

During the holidays, Luna had helped her grandmother Ximiha sell Bombo with peanuts to afford her next tuition fees. But it was during this period that she heard something that would change her perspective: a giant plant, known as Mutumbu, that lived under the scorching sun without water, was being mistreated. This deeply troubled her.

Back at school, in a lesson dedicated to discussing the holidays and the environment, Luna shared her concern about the plant. Her classmates, initially skeptical, learned from the teacher that the Mutumbu, or Welwitschia Mirabilis, was a rare and special plant found only in the Namibe province of Angola. Together, the students decided to write a letter to the Minister of the Environment, asking for protection for this unique plant.

The teacher, always encouraging curiosity and learning, used this opportunity to teach about the importance of environmental conservation. They learned about the plant, measured distances on the map, and gained a deeper understanding of their country's biodiversity. After a week of anxious waiting, they received a response from the ministry, promising measures to protect the Mutumbu.

This story of Luna and her classmates is not just about a plant. It's about responsibility, learning, and the power of children to make a difference. It's a lesson in how, together, we can care for our planet and protect the natural wonders it holds.

# Story Statistics, Detailed Summary

- **Days:** 4
- **Scenes:** 10
- **Locations:** 2
- **Characters:**
    - **Adults:** 1 (Teacher)
        - **Children:** 2 main (Luna, Mateus) + other collective students
- **Dialogue Lines:** 31
- **Paragraphs:** 28
- **Sentences:** 90
- **Verbs:** 103
- **Commas:** 49
- **Periods (Paragraph Endings):** 28
- **Questions:** 8
- **Exclamations:** 6
- **Colons:** 5

# The Girl Who Protected the Great Plant

One day, in a village, there lived a child who cared deeply about everything around her. Her name was Luna.

She loved playing outdoors and helping her grandmother with daily chores. Luna was sad returning to school after the blue summer. She didn't have exciting stories to tell like her other classmates, as she had spent the holidays helping her grandmother Ximiha sell Bombo with peanuts to pay for her upcoming tuition fees.

The next morning, Luna walked slowly to school. The sun was shining in the sky, and the birds were singing, but she couldn't shake the sadness from her heart.

In the classroom, the teacher, always smiling and full of energy, began the lesson: "Today, we're going to talk..."

"...about our holidays and the environment," said the teacher.

Almost all the other students had adventures to share. João talked about his trip to the beach, Maria spoke about her visit to the zoo, and Pedro described his mountain hikes. When it was Luna's turn, she hesitated for a moment, feeling a lump in her throat.

The teacher then turned to Mateus: "You've been quiet for a while. What did you do last summer?"

"I... I didn't do much, Miss," said Mateus, looking uncomfortable. "Actually, I had a lot of stomach aches because I ate too many sweets when I went to help my grandmother Teté make some traditional snacks." The class burst into laughter, teasing him. "Ha ha ha, he had stomach aches!... Greedy Ganga!" shouted João.

"Luna," the teacher called. "How was your summer?"

Luna took a deep breath and began to speak: "I didn't do much either, Miss. But one day, my dad took me to my grandmother's house. While I was there, I heard on the radio that a giant plant, which lives under the sun without water, was mistreated during the summer!"

Her classmates began to tease her. "A giant plant in Angola? How could a plant...

"...survive without water?"

"Quiet, please," the teacher interrupted. "There really is a huge plant in Angola called Welwitschia Mirabilis."

"My grandmother calls It 'Mutumbu,'" said Luna. "It's only found In the Namibe province and nowhere else in the world."

The classroom fell silent as everyone took in this information.

Luna, with tears in her eyes, continued: "I heard that people who visited the area this summer stepped on and even cut parts of the Mutumbu's leaves. I'm afraid it might disappear!"

The teacher, recognising the seriousness of the situation, decided to teach something important. "Do you know who can help us protect the Great Plant?" she asked.

The students thought for a moment. "Maybe the president?" suggested one of them.

"Good attempt, but the one who specifically looks after the environment in our country is the Minister for the Environment," the teacher explained. "Our country has an institution where people work to protect plants, forests, and animals. And the main person responsible for this task is the Minister for the Environment."

Excited by the idea, Luna suggested, "Shall we write a letter to the Minister for the Environment and ask him to protect the Mutumbu?"

"I agree!" all the students said in unison.

"What a great idea, Luna," said the teacher.

"Let's take this opportunity to learn about how to protect our environment and also use our knowledge of Mathematics to understand the importance of quantities and measurements."

# Lesson on the Great Plant

T he following day, the classroom was decorated with maps and images of plants. The teacher brought a large map of Angola and highlighted the Namibe province. "This is where the Mutumbu, or Welwitschia Mirabilis, lives," she explained. "Let's measure the distance between our school and the Namibe province. Who knows how to do that?"

The students began to discuss, using rulers and the scale of the map to calculate the distance. Mateus, focused, did some calculations and said, "It's about 1,200 kilometers!"

"Exactly," said the teacher with a smile. "And do you know why it's important to protect this plant?"

Luna raised her hand and replied, "Because it only exists here and can live for hundreds of years!"

The teacher agreed. "Moreover, it teaches us about resilience and adaptation. Now, let's write our letter to the Minister for the Environment, explaining why the Mutumbu is so important and what we can do to protect it."

The students divided into groups, discussing and writing. It was a lesson full of enthusiasm and collaboration.

A week later, they received a response from the ministry, thanking them for their concern and promising measures to protect the plant.

# Teachings and Conclusion

A few days later, during a Science lesson, the teacher shared the good news with the class. "Mutumbu is saved, at least for now," said Luna, smiling. "But we need to keep learning and taking care of our environment."

"Yes," agreed the teacher. "And remember, protecting nature is everyone's responsibility. You've done a great job starting this initiative."

The students felt proud and motivated to keep making a difference. And so, Luna and her classmates learned a valuable lesson about environmental responsibility and the importance of collaboration.

# Moral of the Story

**Environmental Responsibility:**

The story highlights the importance of caring for the environment and protecting the plants and animals that are part of our ecosystem. Luna and her classmates learn that each of us has a vital role in preserving nature.

**Power of Education:**

The narrative shows how education can be a powerful tool for raising awareness and prompting action. The teacher uses the situation of the Mutumbu plant to teach the students about environmental conservation and citizenship.

## Collective Action:

Luna, along with her classmates, demonstrates that unity and collective action can lead to positive changes. Writing a letter to the Minister of the Environment is an... Example of How Children, Despite Being Young, Can Influence Important Decisions

## Valuing Local Culture:

The story highlights the richness of local biodiversity, such as the Mutumbu plant, which is unique to Angola. This teaches children to value and protect their own natural and cultural heritage.

## Empathy and Concern for Others:

Luna cares deeply about the Mutumbu plant and its preservation. Her empathy extends beyond people, showing that caring for the environment is a way of caring for others.

## Importance of Knowledge and Curiosity:

The story encourages children to be curious and seek knowledge. Luna and her classmates learn not only about the plant but also about geography... Science and Mathematics, Integrating Various Fields of Learning.

## Moral Summary

The moral of the story is that we all have a responsibility to protect the environment and that, through education, collective action, and valuing knowledge, we can make a significant difference. Additionally, the story teaches that empathy and concern for others also include caring for nature, showing that small actions can lead to big changes.

*T*he **Welwitschia mirabilis**, commonly known as Welwitschia or tumboa tree, is a remarkable and unique plant found in the Namib Desert, which spans areas of Angola and Namibia. Here are some scientific and interesting details about this plant:

# Description and Characteristics

## 1. Morphology:

- The Welwitschia mirabilis is known for its unique appearance, with only two large, leathery leaves that grow continuously throughout the plant's life. These leaves extend from a short, broad, woody base.

- The leaves can grow to several metres in length, and as they wear down at the edges, they appear as multiple leaves, but they are actually only two.

## 2. Longevity:

One of the most remarkable characteristics of the Welwitschia is its longevity. It is estimated that some plants can live up to 2,000 years.

## 3. Habitat:

The Welwitschia is adapted to the extreme environment of the Namib Desert, surviving in a region where annual rainfall is very low, and moisture is primarily provided by fog from the Atlantic Ocean.

# Adaptations and Ecology

## 1. Desert Adaptations:

- The plant has a deep root system that allows it to access underground water. Additionally, its leaves are efficient at capturing moisture from the fog, which is crucial for its survival in such an arid environment.

- The Welwitschia also has a cuticle... thick cuticle and adapted stomata to minimise water loss.

## 2. Reproduction:

- The Welwitschia is dioecious, meaning there are separate male and female plants.

- Reproduction occurs through cones, which are pollinated by insects.

# Scientific and Cultural Importance

## 1. Botanical Relic:

- The Welwitschia mirabilis is considered a "living fossil" because it belongs to a very ancient group of plants dating back to the Jurassic period. It is the only existing species in the Welwitschiaceae family.

## 2. Cultural and Medicinal:

- In local culture, especially among the indigenous peoples of Namibe, the plant is known as "tumboa" and holds cultural and symbolic significance. In some traditions, parts of the plant are used for medicinal purposes.

## Research and Scientific Studies

## 1. Genetics and Evolution:

- Genetic studies of the Welwitschia have provided insights into the evolution of gymnosperms. Its genome reveals unique adaptations to its desert habitat.

## 2. Physiology and Resilience:

- Research on the physiology of Welwitschia mirabilis shows how it can survive in extreme conditions, offering models to study the resilience and adaptability of plants in arid environments.

# Notable Scientific Articles

1. **"Welwitschia mirabilis: The Desert Enigma"**

   - This article explores the ecology...

   *Physiology and Genetics of the Plant, Detailing How It Has Adapted to Extreme Desert Conditions*

**2.** *Genomic Adaptations in Welwitschia mirabilis* – Focused on genetic discoveries, this study highlights how the plant has developed unique mechanisms to survive in an environment with limited water.

**3.** *Longevity and Growth Patterns in Welwitschia mirabilis* – Examining growth patterns and longevity, the article discusses how the plant can live for millennia and continue to grow throughout its life. Welwitschia mirabilis remains the subject of intense scientific research due to its unique characteristics and remarkable adaptations, making it a fascinating model for studies on survival in extreme conditions and plant evolution.

# Friedrich Welwitsch

**Article**   **Talk**

🗛                                    ☆   ✏

**Friedrich Martin Josef Welwitsch** (25 February 1806 – 20 October 1872) was an Austrian explorer and botanist who in Angola was the first European to describe the plant *Welwitschia mirabilis*. His report received wide attention among the botanists and general public, comparable only to the discovery of two other plants in the 19th century, namely *Victoria amazonica* and *Rafflesia arnoldii*.[1]

**Friedrich Martin Josef Welwitsch**

# Color Me

Color me

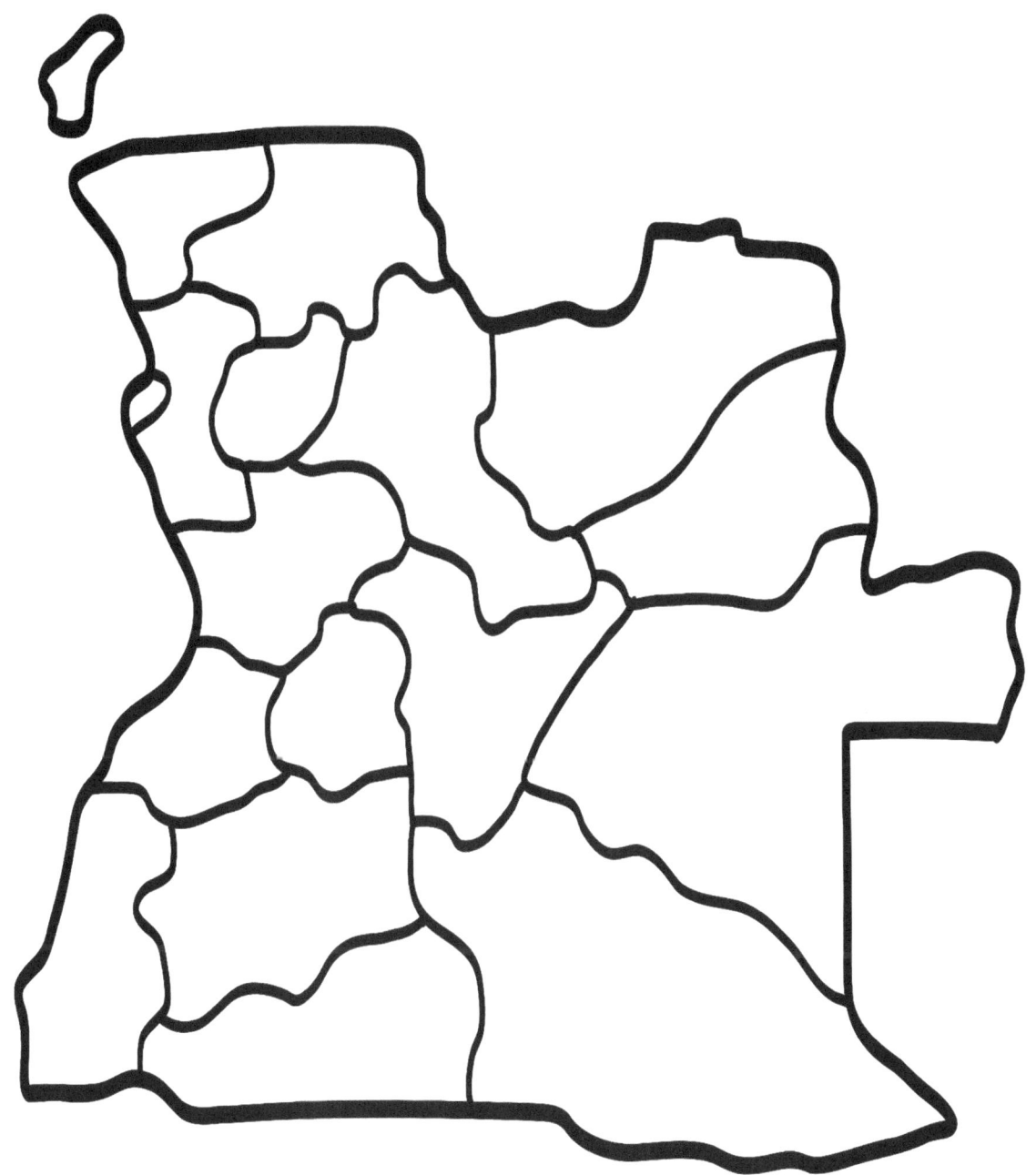

My Llibrary
@mylibrary70

TikTok

Copy link    Share link

https://www.instagram.com/_manu.santana

# ABOUT THE AUTHOR

I am Maria Santana, an Angolan writer residing in London.

I am here to take you on this emotional journey through this book.

As a child, I loved children's books such as Cinderella, Puss in Boots, and Anita and the Dog, but at that time, there were only European children's books, and there were no books that portrayed African stories and tales.

This left a void, but it never stopped me from reading.

I love reading and have always read to my children, and today I read to my grandchildren and godchildren. As an author, I write out of love for African culture, more specifically Angolan culture, as it serves as a guardian of the values and traditions that fuel the imagination of Angolan children and youth.

This inspired me to write the book The Most Coveted Sable Antelope of Angola, so that our children can create unforgettable memories with an original story about their culture and learn how rich it truly is.

Thank you!

Princesa Luna

www.ingramcontent.com/pod-product-compliance
Lightning Source LLC
Chambersburg PA
CBHW041431120626
46547CB00002B/169